TABLE OF CONTENTS

DISCLAIMER AND TERMS OF USE AGREEMENT:

Introduction – Protecting Your Business from Cyber Criminals

Chapter 1 – The Problem is Organized

Chapter 2 – The Solution is Organized too!

Chapter 3 – How to Spot Cyber Crime Activity

Chapter 4 – I Have a Special Gift for My Readers

Meet the Author

Cyber Protect Your Business
Protecting Your Business from Cyber Criminals
©Copyright 2012 by Dr. Leland Benton

DISCLAIMER AND TERMS OF USE AGREEMENT:

(Please Read This Before Using This Book)

This information is for educational and informational purposes only. The content is not intended to be a substitute for any professional advice, diagnosis, or treatment.

The author and publisher of this book and the accompanying materials have used their best efforts in preparing this book.

The author and publisher make no representation or warranties with respect to the accuracy, applicability, fitness, or completeness of the contents of this book. The information contained in this book is strictly for educational purposes. Therefore, if you wish to apply ideas contained in this book, you are taking full responsibility for your actions.

The author and publisher disclaim any warranties (express or implied), merchantability, or fitness for any particular purpose. The author and publisher shall in no event be held liable to any party for any direct, indirect, punitive, special, incidental or other consequential damages arising directly or indirectly from any use of this material, which is provided "as is", and without warranties. As always, the advice of a competent legal, tax, accounting, medical or other professional should be sought where applicable.

The author and publisher do not warrant the performance, effectiveness or applicability of any sites listed or linked to in this book. All links are for information purposes only and are not warranted for content, accuracy or any other implied or explicit purpose. No part of this may be copied, or changed in any format, or used in any way other than what is outlined within this course under any circumstances. Violators will be prosecuted.

This book is © Copyrighted by ePubWealth.com.

** Bonus **
Watch our FREE 56-minute ForensicsNation Online Public Awareness Seminar that will truly open your eyes to what you are facing with cyber crime. Go here to view the view the seminar: http://www.AddMeInNow.com

---

Introduction – Protecting Your Business from Cyber Criminals

"Tell me; where is cyberspace? Point out to me exactly where it is. Show me the billion of airwaves coursing through our bodies and surroundings non-stop 24/7.

You have a website? Reach out and touch it for me. Reach out and pluck a fax from the air. Or reach out and pluck the photo of your kid that you just sent grandma out of the air and show it to me.

Where is the Internet? And where are the billions of bits of information sent at seemingly light speed around the world. Show them to me.

The text message you sent...where did it go and how did it get there? Show me the software you just downloaded and installed on your computer. Not the interface that pops up on your computer screen but show me the bits and bytes that make it work.

It is all AIR!!! It is nothing more than air. Every day we all buy, send and use air and every day we all do not realize that our lives are changing as new technology is released and as becomes a major part of our lives."

And sometimes the air is polluted!

Give me 30-minutes and I can turn your life into a living HELL

In 30-minutes I can:

- Access your bank accounts and steal your money
- Tap your cell phone; listen to your phone calls, read your text messages.
- I can track your movements using GPS
- I can learn all about you – where you live, where you work, your habits, if you are single or married, your kid's names and ages, EVERYTHING!
- I can access your social media and change your profile and pics
- I can post false information about you that will never come off the net.
- I can find out your religious affiliation, voting records, and more.
- I will know your car, license info, and insurance data.

In short, give me 30-minutes and I will know everything about you and you cannot stop me because all of this info is on the Internet and you will never know it is me because I can hide where nobody will find me.

Computer vs. Internet Forensics

The widespread use of computer forensics resulted from the convergence of two factors: the increasing dependence of law enforcement on computing (as in the area of fingerprints) and the ubiquity of computers that followed from the microcomputer revolution. As computer forensics evolved, it was modeled after the basic investigative methodologies of law enforcement and the security industry that championed its use.

Not surprisingly, computer forensics is about the "preservation, identification, extraction, documentation and interpretation of computer data." In order to accomplish these goals, there are well-defined procedures, also derived from law enforcement, for acquiring and analyzing the evidence without damaging it and authenticating the evidence and providing a chain-of-custody that will hold up in court.

The tools for the "search-and-seizure" side of computer forensics are a potpourri of sophisticated tools that are primarily focused on the physical side of computing: i.e., tracing and locating computer hardware, recovering hidden data from storage media, identifying and recovering hidden data, decrypting files, decompressing data, cracking passwords, "crowbarring" an operating system (bypassing normal security controls and permissions), and so forth. For those who are old enough to remember the original Norton Utilities for DOS think of these modern tools as the original Norton Disk Editor for DOS on steroids.

Listed below are some common categories and a few examples of computer forensics toolkits:

- File Viewers: Quick View Plus (http://www.jasc.com)
- Image Viewers: ThumbsPlus http://www.cerious.com)
- Password Crackers: l0phtcrack or LC4 (http://www.atstake.com)

- Format-independent Text Search: dtsearch (http://www.dtsearch.com)
- Drive Imaging: Norton Utilities' Ghost (http://www.symantec.com)
- Complete Computer Forensics Toolkits:
- Forensics Toolkit (http://www.foundstone.com);
- ForensiX (http://www.all.net);
- EnCase Forensic (http://www.encase.com)
- Forensic Computer Systems: Forensic-Computers (http://www.forensic-computers.com)
- One of the more full-featured network tools, NetScanTools Pro (http://www.netscantools.com) Note the abundance of features built into one product!

Internet Forensics specialist uses many of the same tools and engages in the same set of practices as the person he/she is investigating. Let me illustrate with a few examples. Suppose that you've received some suspicious email, and want to verify the authenticity of a URL included within. A number of options are available. One might use a browser to access information from the American Registry for Internet Numbers (http://www.arin.net). Or one might use any number of OS utilities. But we'll save ourselves some time and worry, and use a general network appliance, NetScanTools Pro. We identified the registration, domain name servers, currency information, etc. for netscantools.com.

Now let's change the scenario slightly. Suppose that we had some hostile intent, and wanted to ferret out information about some company's network infrastructure. What tool might we use? You guessed it, NetScanTools Pro. The point is that the self-same tool is equally useful to the hacker conducting basic network reconnaissance and the legitimate Internet security specialist who's trying to determine whether a URL links to a legitimate company or a packet "booby trap." The point is that, both uses require essentially the same skill sets.

In Internet Forensics it is customarily the case that the forensic specialist undergoes the same level of education and training as the hacker he or she seeks to thwart. The difference is one of ethics, not skill. We observed that this was not true of the perpetrator and investigator in computer forensics.

To drive home the point, look at the other options that NetScanTools Pro provides. One can use an ICMP "ping" to identify whether a particular network host is online just as easily as one can use it to identify activity periods in network reconnaissance or a network topology. One can use a Traceroute to determine network bottlenecks, or to identify intervening routers and gateways for possible man-in-the-middle attacks. One can use Port Probe to verify that a firewall is appropriately configured, or to make a list of vulnerable services on a host that may be exploited.

Where computer forensics deals with physical things, Internet forensics deals with the ephemeral. The computer forensics specialist at least has something to seize and investigate. The Internet forensics specialist only has something to investigate if the packet filters, firewalls and intrusion detection systems were set up to anticipate the breach of security. But, if one could always anticipate the breach, one could always block it. Therein lays the art, and the mystery.

If I've been successful, I've got you thinking about the fundamental differences between computer forensics and internet forensics. I think that on careful analysis, one has to conclude (a) that these are fundamentally different skills, (b) that in the case of Internet forensics, the skill sets of the successful perpetrator and successful investigator are pretty much the same, and (c) Internet forensics is as much a discipline as its search-and-seizure counterpart. This validity of these conclusions may be confirmed in any number of ways. For the most part the tools-of-the-trade for both hacker and Internet forensics specialist are the same, though the occasional extreme case like Dug Song's Dsniff http://monkey.org/~dugsong/dsniff challenges this generalization. It's hard for me to imagine a legitimate, lawful use of Dsniff's "macof" utility that enables the users to flood switch state tables! But in the main, the hacker and the Internet Forensics specialist could co-exist with the same tools and equipment.

Statistics on Internet Fraud

The Internet Crime Complaint Center (IC3), a joint venture of the FBI and the National White Collar Crime Center found:

- Online auction fraud was the most reported type of fraud and accounted for 44.9% of consumers' complaints

- Non-delivered merchandise and/or payment made up 19.0% of complaints

- Check fraud represented 4.9% of complaints

- About 70% of the fraud victims were scammed through www (e.g. online auctions)

- About 30% of the victims were scammed by emails

Payment Methods

Top methods of payment used by victims of Internet fraud include: Wire, Credit Card, Bank Debit, Money Order, and Check

The average loss for all Internet frauds was $1,500. More than half of these losses occurred through auctions. So protect yourself from becoming the next victim of an auction fraud. Read the tips on how to prevent auction frauds from happening to you.

Tips on How to Prevent Auction Frauds

- Learn as much as you can from the seller

- Read and examine the feedback on the seller

- Check the location of the seller. If the seller is abroad and a problem arises it will be harder to solve.

- Ask if shipping and delivery are included in the price so you receive no unexpected or additional costs.

- Refuse to give the seller your social security number or driver's license number to prevent identity theft. In fact get used to saying "no" to information requests on the Internet.

How do hackers and crackers do it?

With the advent of the internet, online information is becoming more and more prevalent without the person or entity even knowing their information is listed online.

Two of the main culprits are the following:

1. Epsilon: http://www.epsilon.com

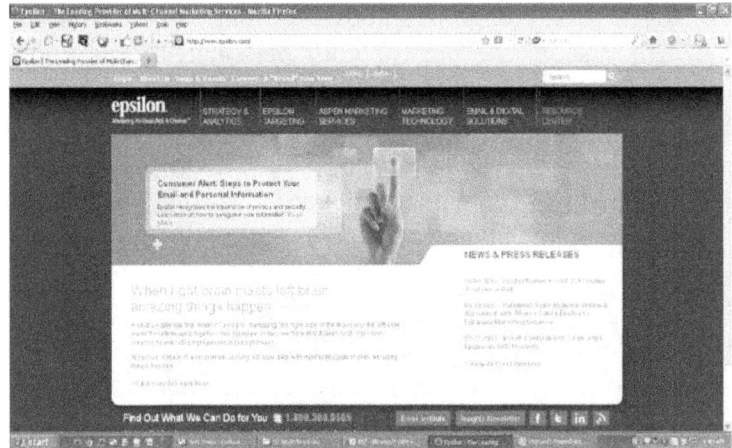

2. Acxiom: http://www.acxiom.com

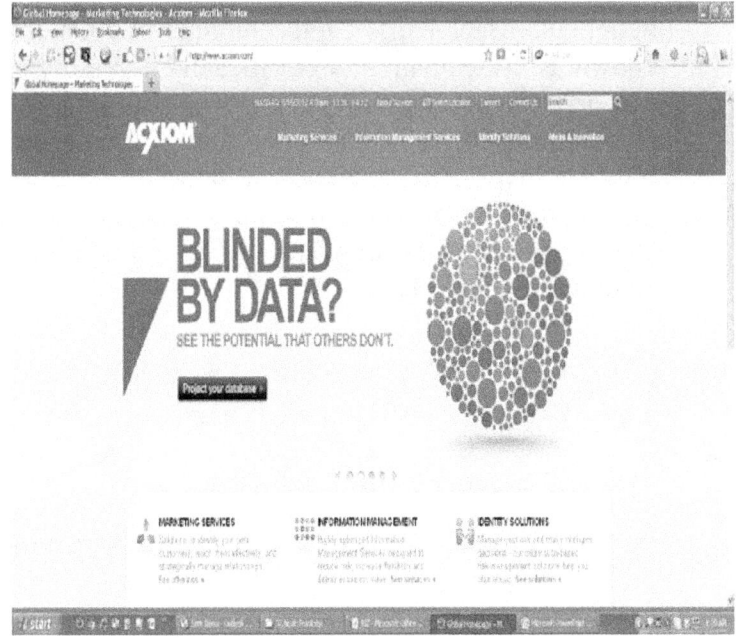

The two companies above are called "data miners" and they scour the net for your personal information. They then sell this information to mostly legitimate businesses seeking to sell you goods and services but they also sell to hackers and crackers. No, not on purpose; they are duped just like you but nevertheless they do sell your info to people who should not have it.

People like Hackman1...in the summer of 2008, a hacker known as "Hackman1" began illegally accessing various corporate databases and stealing personal and financial data in order to commit identity theft. In the course of a 6-month investigation, he was responsible for over 5566 victims totaling over $15-million in damages. When he was apprehended, he was on a yacht off the Florida Keys committing more identity theft.

How bad is it? Listen…

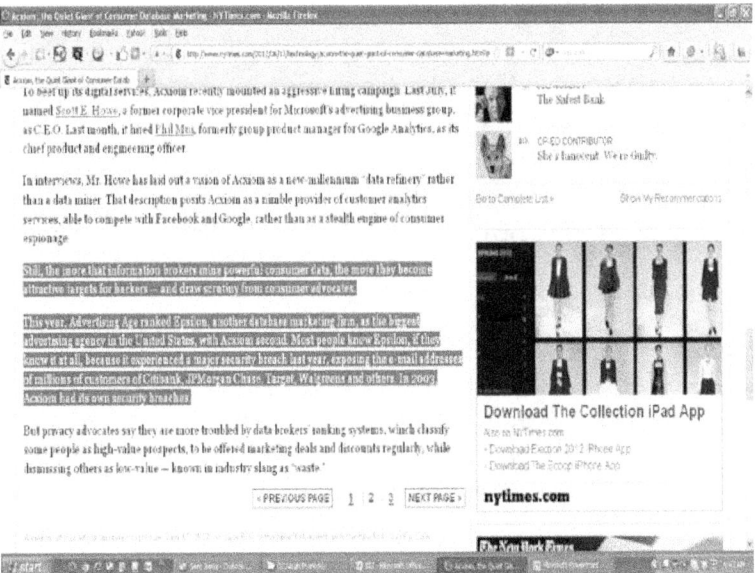

Now let's dig deeper into the problem.

Chapter 1 – The Problem is Organized

Most cyber-crime is conducted by 10-worldwide gangs.

The 10-Most Notorious Cyber Gangs

1-Russian Business Network
2-Rock Phish Gang
3-NSA
4-Grey Pigeon Authors
5-Stormworm Gang
6-Awola Crew
7-DRG Group
8-South American Groups
9-Oga-Nigerian
10-Individual Hackers (Anonymous)

As cyber-crime increases, so does their income and this feeds the increase of more cyber-crime.

Like drugs, cyber-crime pays and it pays very well.

Corporate Espionage is the most cyber-criminal activity and at the same time, the least protected area of vulnerability. And it is not being conducted just by nation-states against USA businesses either. The Gang of 10 hacking organizations cost American businesses an estimated $2-billion every year.

The New York Times

False Tax Returns
With Personal Data in Hand, Thieves File Early and Often

MIAMI — Besieged by identity theft, Florida now faces a fast-spreading form of fraud so simple and lucrative that some violent criminals have traded their guns for laptops. And the target is the United States Treasury.

J. Russell George, the Treasury inspector general for tax administration, testified before Congress this month that the I.R.S. detected 940,000 fake returns for 2010 in which identity thieves would have received $6.5 billion in refunds. But Mr. George said the agency missed an additional 1.5 million returns with possibly fraudulent refunds worth more than $5.2 billion.

From 2008 to 2011, the number of returns filed by identity thieves and stopped by the I.R.S. increased significantly, officials said. Last year, it was at least 1.3 million, said Steven T. Miller, deputy commissioner for services and enforcement at the agency. This year, with only 30 percent of the filings reviewed so far, the number is already at 2.6 million. The bulk is related to identity theft, Mr. Miller said.

Teen recounts horror of abduction into sex slavery
Many young victims of human traffickers treated as criminals themselves

For someone who's only 18, Shauna Newell is remarkably composed as she describes being kidnapped, drugged, gang-raped and savagely beaten. It is only when she talks about seeing one of the men who sexually assaulted her — free and unafraid of being prosecuted — that she starts to break down.

"I went out to the beach a few weeks ago and I saw the dude who raped me, and he just looked at me," Newell told NBC News, her voice choking. "Like, hey ... you ruined my whole life. You have scared me for the rest of my life and you're just sitting there going on with your life like nothing is wrong."

Child Abduction

FHP - *Mall* & Shopping Safety
www.flhsmv.gov/fhp/misc/christmas/mst.htm

More than 100000 *children* are *abducted* every year -- often in *malls* or department stores, according to the National Center for Missing and Exploited *Children*...

The day I was almost *abducted* & killed by a *child* predator - Kanuk...
http://open.salon.com/blog/kanuk/2010/06/22/the_day_i_was_almost_abducted_killed_by_a_child_predator
Jun 22, 2010 – The day I was almost *abducted* & killed by a *child* predator ... So I went on my way and walked to the *mall's* record store. Remember those?

Is a fifth grader old enough to go to the *mall* by himself?
http://www.wiki.answers.com
And don't forget that even adult women have been *kidnapped from malls*, as well as other public places, so why would you think your *child* would be an exception...

SulphurDailyNews.com

Dreamboard

This week, the United States Attorney joined forces with the Attorney General and Department of Homeland Security to announce the largest United States prosecution of an international criminal network.

What's even worse about this particular case ... **the criminal organization was developed to sexually exploit children.**

Dating back to December of 2009, the investigation targeted 72 defendants and more than 500 individuals around the world for their participation in an online organization called, **"Dreamboard." This private, members-only online bulletin board was created and operated to promote pedophilia and encourage the sexual abuse of very young children.**

If you have young children, you may want to pay close attention to the particulars of this case. Let us warn you, however, it's not pleasant, but it's reality.

It gets worse…

The Daily Dot
Today on the Web

¡Viva Anonymous! The hacker gang is back in Mexico

"I strongly doubt the kidnapping took place," said [ ] the chief forensics investigator for ForensicsNation, wh hackers and groups like Anonuymous. "The cartel are r Anonymous."

THE WALL STREET JOURNAL

'Stingray' Phone Tracker Fuels Constitutional Clash

The New York Times

Justices Say GPS Tracker Violated Privacy Rights

NEWS

LulzSec 'Leader' Turns on Fellow Hacktivists:Feds

The Washington Post

The Feds concerned about hackers opening Prison doors

The New York Times

In Attack on Vatican Web Site, a Glimpse of Hackers' Tactics

YAHOO! NEWS

Minnesota Wi-Fi hacker gets 18 years in prison for terrorizing neighbors

theguardian

Feds versus the hacker underground: army of informers turned by fear

Mail Online

And then you have what is being called "Not-So Legal Hacking of your personal info

Sinister truth about Google spies: Street View cars stole information from British households but executives 'covered it up' for years. Work of Street View cars to be examined over allegations Google used them to download personal details - Emails, texts, photos and documents taken from Wi-Fi networks as cars photographed British roads. Engineer who designed software said a privacy lawyer should be consulted

Microsoft

ebaY

lendio

Mail Online

Even the government is spying on you...if you use certain words. Revealed: Hundreds of words to avoid using online if you don't want the government spying on you (and they include 'pork', 'cloud' and 'Mexico'). Department of Homeland Security forced to release list following freedom of information request. Agency insists it only looks for evidence of genuine threats to the U.S. and not for signs of general dissent. The words are included in the department's 2011 'Analyst's Desktop Binder' used by workers at their National Operations Center which instructs workers to identify 'media reports that reflect adversely on DHS and response activities'.

Cyber Criminals are Organized

Hackers have their own news organization, their own news network. They even have their own education system and even their own movie. What's next? Locusts? Boils?

Actually the Hacker Underground is complete with their own news sites, news networks and these are really good things. These sites are where hackers BUY their information from other hackers. Info such as identity theft financial records, social security numbers, etc.

So, we pose as buyers or sellers and "bait" the hackers. When they respond we plant a tracking bug into their computer systems and instantly they go into our databases.

Now you may ask how do hackers pay for this information without revealing their identities. They use companies like Xoom.com…no questions asked, the hacker bank…but even their systems are not that secure (lol). They also use companies like Payza, because it is offshore and outside the regulations of The Patriot Act.

Hackers teach other hackers. Look...

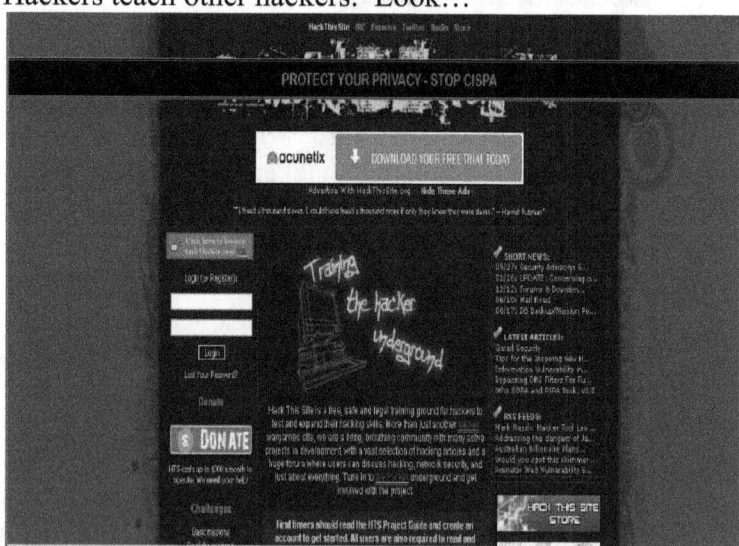

CISPA means the "Cyber Intelligence Sharing and Protection Act"

How To Become A Hacker
Eric Steven Raymond

Table of Contents

Why This Document?
What Is a Hacker?
The Hacker Attitude
    1. The world is full of fascinating problems waiting to be solved.
    2. No problem should ever have to be solved twice.
    3. Bordom and drudgery are evil.
    4. Freedom is good.
    5. Attitude is no substitute for competence.
Basic Hacking Skills
    1. Learn how to program
    2. Get one of the open-source Unixes and learn to use and run it.
    3. Learn how to use the World Wide Web and write HTML.
    4. If you don't have functional English, learn it.
Status in the Hacker Culture
    1. Write open-source software
    2. Help test and debug open-source software
    3. Publish useful information
    4. Help keep the infrastructure working
    5. Serve the hacker culture itself
The Hacker/Nerd Connection
Points For Style
Historical Note: Hacking, Open Source and Free Software

#1 Target of Hackers and Crackers
LAW ENFORCEMENT

#2 Target of Hackers and Crackers - YOU!

Hackers and Crackers go after YOU in this order of importance

1. Children – predators are most active in child abduction and abuse.
2. Women – everything from stalking to voyeurism to sex slavery.
3. Businesses – small business are more often targeted due to less protective measures.
4. General Population – in the form of various cyber crimes such as identity theft, computer intrusion, and phishing scams.
5. Government Agencies – patient records on file with state record keepers getting hacked.

Areas of Personal EXPOSURE

- Credit Card Fraud
- Identity Theft
- Financial Scams
- Child Predation
- Computer Hijacking
- Malware, Spyware
- Electronic Voyeurism
- Viruses
- Keystroke Logging
- Phishing
- User Account & Password Theft
- Cell Phone Spying
- Online Auction Fraud – Ebay, etc.
- And much more…

The above areas of personal exposure are the more prevalent forms of cyber crimes directed against individuals. It is by no means a complete list.

The main problem is that the average computer user has no idea that they are exposed and even if they do, they have no idea how to protect themselves.

As technology expands, the tools available to the hacker and cyber-criminal expand too. They keep up with everything on the Internet where the average user does not.

Cyber-criminals are organizing into gangs. The most famous is the hacking gang called Anonymous that used "Denial of Service" techniques against major financial institutions that denied Wikileaks merchant account facilities in 2011.

But in countries such as Russia and many of the old "iron curtain" countries too, organized cyber-crime gangs are increasing.

Chapter 2 – The Solution is Organized too!

The following Corporate Checklist is designed to identify the main and common areas of vulnerability and upon completion of the Checklist, a ForensicsNation security consultant will analyze each participating business and do an in depth analysis of specific vulnerabilities.

Corporate Checklist

Part 1: The hacker subculture and approach
- An overview of the risks and threats
- An insight into the hacker underground
- The anatomy of a hack

Part 2: TCP/IP fundamentals
- TCP/IP and its relevance to hacking
- TCP header, flags and options

- UDP, ICMP and ARP
- Network traffic dump analysis
- Class exercises and lab sessions

Part 3: Reconnaissance techniques
- Selecting a target
- Identifying target hosts and services
- Network mapping techniques
- Fingerprinting and OS determination
- Scanning and stealth techniques
- Class exercises and lab sessions

Part 4: Compromising networks
- Vulnerability cross referencing
- Code auditing and insecure code examples
- Exploiting network services
- Sniffers, backdoors and root kits
- Trojans and session hijacking
- Denial of service attacks
- Trust exploitation and spoofing
- Buffer overflow techniques
- Web page graffiti attacks
- War dialers and dial-in hacking
- Manipulating audit trails and security logs
- Class exercises and lab sessions

Part 5: Windows Applied Hacking
- Windows components, Domains and structures
- Remote information gathering
- Scanning and banner checking
- Selecting services to attack
- Enumerating Windows information
- Windows hacking techniques

- Recent Windows vulnerabilities
- Class exercises and lab sessions

Part 6: Windows effective countermeasures
- User account policies and group allocations
- File and directory permissions
- File and print shares
- Hardening the registry
- Domains and trust relationships
- Securing network services
- Windows antivirus strategies
- Windows and Internet security
- Windows auditing and security logs
- Windows service packs and hot fixes
- Class exercises and lab sessions

Part 7: Unix applied hacking
- Unix components
- Unix variants
- Remote and local information gathering
- Scanning and fingerprinting
- Selecting services to attack
- Unix hacking techniques
- Recent Unix vulnerabilities
- Class exercises and lab sessions

Part 8: Unix effective countermeasures
- Unix password and group files
- User account and password controls
- Controlling command line access
- File and directory permissions
- SUID and SGID controls
- Crontab security

- Network and trust relationships
- Securing network services
- Unix antivirus strategies
- Unix and Internet security
- Unix auditing and security logs
- Unix security patches
- Class exercises and lab sessions

Part 9: Network security strategies
- Risk management and AS/NZS 4360
- Security management and AS/NZS 7799
- Developing a practical security strategy
- Physical security and environmental controls
- Personnel security and awareness training
- Firewall risks and strategies
- Intrusion detection system risks and strategies
- An overview of ecommerce security issues
- An overview of wireless security issues
- An overview of PBX security issues
- An overview of intrusion analysis techniques
- An overview of forensics procedures
- An overview of IT contingency planning
- Class exercises and lab sessions

Part 10: Advanced Security Techniques
*Inventory of Authorized and Unauthorized Devices
*Inventory of Authorized and Unauthorized Software
*Secure Configurations for Hardware and Software on Laptops, Workstations, and Servers
*Continuous Vulnerability Assessment and Remediation
*Malware Defenses
*Application Software Security
*Wireless Device Control

*Data Recovery Capability
*Security Skills Assessment and Appropriate Training to Fill Gaps
*Secure Configurations for Network Devices such as Firewalls, Routers, and Switches
*Limitation and Control of Network Ports, Protocols, and Services
*Controlled Use of Administrative Privileges
*Boundary Defense
*Maintenance, Monitoring, and Analysis of Security Audit Logs
*Controlled Access Based on the Need to Know
*Account Monitoring and Control
*Data Loss Prevention
*Incident Response Capability
*Secure Network Engineering
*Penetration Tests and Red Team Exercises

Prevention is the answer and by analyzing your vulnerabilities before cyber criminals strike, you can prevent some undeserved heartache and loss of assets.

Chapter 3 – How to Spot Cyber Crime Activity

The following was written by A.J. Surin and although he is writing to a Malaysian audience, what he writes applies to the United States too. The complete White Paper can be found here:

http://www.crime-research.org/library/Cybercriminal.html

To catch a cybercriminal
By A.J. Surin

WHAT is cybercrime? The Oxford Reference Online defines cybercrime as crime committed over the Internet

http://www.oxfordreference.com/views/ENTRY.html?ssid=175131518&entry=t49.000925&srn=1&category=-FIRSTHIT

Some people call cybercrime "computer crime." The Encyclopedia Britannica defines computer crime as any crime that is committed by means of special knowledge or expert use of computer technology.

Computer crime could reasonably include a wide variety of criminal offences, activities, or issues. The scope of the definition becomes even larger with the frequent companion or substitute term "computer-related crime." Some writers are also of the opinion that "computer crime" refers to computer-related activities which are either criminal in the legal sense of the word or just antisocial behavior where there is no breach of the law (Lee, M.K.O. (1995) Legal control of computer crime in Hong Kong, Information Management & Computer Security 3(2) 13-19 – http://mustafa.emeraldlibrary.com/vl=4775179/cl=50/nw=1/rpsv/~1177/v3n2/s3/p13).

The word "hacker" should also be defined here, as it will be used extensively in this article – hackers are basically people who break into and tamper with computer information systems. The word "cracker" carries a similar meaning, and "cracking" means to decipher a code, password or encrypted message.

What is concerning is that organized crime is escalating on the Internet, according to a 2002 statement by the head of Britain's National High-tech Crime Unit, Lee Hynds (www.ananova.com/news/story/sm_724492.html?menu). According to him the Internet provides organized crime groups with "a relatively low risk theatre of operations."

As the topic of cybercrime is so wide, what I would like to do is focus on Malaysia's Computer Crimes Act 1997, local law enforcement and practical tips on how to prevent cybercrime.

Computer crime laws in other countries, the enforcement and multilateral efforts to harmonies laws against cybercrime will be discussed in next month's column.

Are there laws in Malaysia to prosecute cybercriminals? What are the penalties for cybercriminals in Malaysia?

The need for laws against cybercriminals is obvious. A school dropout from the Philippines who wrote the ILOVEYOU virus was not prosecuted by the Philippine Government because at that time, the country did not have laws relating to virus creators. Ironically, the then President Estrada stated that perhaps the Philippines should leverage on the fact that they have such good virus writers to attract global technology companies to base themselves in the Philippines, considering the capable talent available in the country.

Viruses and worms are getting more insidious nowadays – take for instance, the Swen worm, which cleverly disguises itself as an e-mail message from Microsoft with a patch attached.

Illegal uses

Besides hacking and cracking, technology and the Internet can be used for a myriad of other illegal purposes: drug dealers use encrypted fax machines to send orders for narcotics to their suppliers in a neighboring country.

Gangsters can use computers for extortion. Prostitution rings maintain their customer payments and client lists through computer software applications. Burglary rings track break-ins and then inventory their winnings from each job. Gangsters who want to murder a person in hospital can crack the hospital's computers to alter the dosage of medication

http://www.scmagazine.com/scmagazine/2000_04/cover/cover.html

Cybercriminals can range from teenagers who vandalize websites to terrorists who target a nation. However, we will leave the discussion on cyberterrorism to another installation of this column.
Laws specifically catered for criminal activity through, over and using the Internet is essential for a nation state to have, especially in this globalised, Internet age. Take the example of the ILOVEYOU virus again, which spread to at least 45 million computers worldwide causing billions of dollars in damage.

http://www.ananova.com/news/story/sm_51942.html

The Computer Crimes Act 1997 provides for offences against cybercrime. Now, it is not the case that the other Acts of Parliament do not provide for criminal offences (like the Communications and Multimedia Act 1998, the Digital Signature Act 1997 and the Optical Discs Act 2000), it is just that in terms of cybercrime itself, the Act of Parliament which is the most relevant is the Computer Crimes Act. This Act is divided into three parts that is the "Preliminary," "Offences" and "Ancillary and General Provisions" parts and is 12 sections long. It came into force on June 1, 2000.

Section 3 provides for the offence of unauthorized access to computer material. A person shall be guilty of an offence if three elements exist, that is:

- He causes a computer to perform any function with intent to secure access to any program or data held in any computer;
- The access he intends to secure is unauthorized; and
- He knows at the time that he accesses the computer without authorization.

The section then states that the intent a person has to have to commit the offence need not be directed at any particular program or data, a program or data of any particular kind or a program or data held in any particular computer. One meaning of this part may be that it does not matter whether or not a hacker knows what the consequences of his act will be, which program or data he or she will access or even which computer he or she will access, just as long as he knows that his access is unauthorized. The penalty for this offence is a maximum fine of RM 50,000, a maximum prison sentence of five years or both the fine and imprisonment.

Section 4 provides for the offence of unauthorized access with intent to commit or facilitate the commission of a further offence. A person shall be guilty of an offence under this section if two elements exist, that is:

- He or she accesses unauthorized computer material without access; and
- He or she accesses this computer material with the intent of: committing an offence involving fraud or dishonesty or which causes injury as defined in the Penal Code; or facilitating the commission of such an offence whether by himself or by any other person.

A person guilty of an offence under this section shall on conviction be liable to a maximum fine of RM 150,000 or a maximum prison term of 10 years or both the fine and imprisonment. As you can see, the legislature has provided for a higher fine and a higher prison term for this offence, as the crime here is more serious than in Section 3, as the commission of a further offence of fraud, dishonesty or injury is envisaged.

Unauthorized modification

Section 5 provides for the offence of unauthorized modification of the contents of any computer. A person shall be guilty of the offence if he does any act which he knows will cause unauthorized modification of the contents of any computer. Section 5 also states that it is immaterial that the act in question is not directed at any particular program or data a program or data of any kind or a program or data held in any particular computer.

This most probably means that it does not matter whether or not the hacker knows which program or data, or even which computer will be affected by his actions, just as long as he knows his actions will cause unauthorized modifications. For the purposes of Section 5, it is immaterial whether an unauthorized modification is, or is intended to be, permanent or merely temporary. The penalty is a maximum fine of RM 100,000 or a maximum prison sentence of seven years or both the fine and prison sentence. However, if the modification was done to cause injury, then the maximum fine is RM 150,000 and the maximum prison term is 10 years.

Section 6 is the offence of wrongful communication. A person shall be guilty of an offence if he communicates directly or indirectly a number, code, password or other means of access to a computer to any person other than a person to whom he is duly authorized to communicate it to. The penalty for the offence is a maximum fine of RM 25,000 or a maximum prison sentence of three years or both.

Section 7 provides for a criminal offence if a person assists in the commissioning of any of the offences above, attempts to commit any of the offences above or was preparing to commit any of the offences above.

Section 11 provides for the criminal offence if:

- A person assaults, obstructs, hinders or delays a police officer when the latter is attempting to enter any premises for the purposes searching, seizing or arresting as provided for under the Act; or

- A person fails to comply with any lawful demands of a police officer acting in the execution of his duty under the Act.

A person found guilty under Section 11 faces a maximum fine of RM 25,000 or a maximum prison term of three years or to both the fine and prison term.

Section 9 of the Computer Crimes Act states that the provisions of the Act shall have effect outside as well as within Malaysia and where the commission of the offence was performed outside Malaysia, he may be dealt with in respect of such offence as if it was committed at a place within Malaysia. Section 9 goes on to state that the Act shall apply if, for the offence in question, the computer, program or data was in Malaysia or capable of being connected to or sent to or used by or with a computer in Malaysia at the material time.

This practically means that the Computer Crimes Act has extra-territorial jurisdiction – the law can be enforced against an alleged offender even if he is in another country.

One more interesting thing about the Act is that Section 10 gives the power to any police officer to arrest without warrant any person whom he (the police officer) reasonably believes to have committed or is committing an offence under the Act.

Thus, the police have sweeping powers of arrest with regards to cybercrime and reflect the legislature's consideration that it viewed the offences in the Act as pretty serious.

Practical examples of cybercrime

Some people may argue that there is a difference between hackers who break into a website to deface its homepage and cyberterrorists who go to these same websites with the purpose of causing harm to people and damage to databases and information systems (see for instance Lee, M.K.O. (1995) above). However, if you look at Section 5 of the Act carefully, Malaysian law does not make a distinction between a harmless hacker who defaces a webpage and a cyberterrorist who desires to cause injury – both will be guilty of offences under the Act, and both will be punishable, although by different sections of the Act.

Practical examples of cybercrimes include but are not limited to:

Cyberstalking. The goal of a cyberstalker is control. Stalking and harassment over cyberspace is more easily practiced than in real life. There are many cases where cyberstalking crosses over to physical stalking.

Some examples of computer harassment are:

- Live chat obscenities and harassment;
- Unsolicited and threatening e-mail;
- Hostile postings about someone;
- Spreading vicious rumors about someone;
- Leaving abusive messages on a website's guest books.

Cases where the crime can occur even if there was no computer – however, the use of technology makes the commission of the crime faster and permits the processing of larger amounts of information. Examples would be credit card fraud, drug trafficking, criminal breach of trust, forgery, cheating, illegal betting or gambling, forgery of valuable documents (money, checks, passports and identification cards) and money laundering. In the past, the Malaysian Police has investigated rumour mongering and defamation on the Internet.

Malicious codes like worms, viruses and Trojan horses: These exploit security vulnerabilities of a system and they tend to alter or destroy data. The damage they cost is worth millions of Ringgit to companies as well as government agencies. Worms are different from viruses because they are able to spread themselves with no user interaction. A virus can attack systems in many ways: by erasing files, corrupting databases and destroying hard disk drives.

Hacking: Hacked systems can be used for information gathering, information alteration, and sabotage. Vulnerabilities exist in almost every network. Hackers sometime crack into systems to brag about their abilities to penetrate into systems, but others do it for illegal gain or other malicious purposes. Today, hacking is simpler than ever – hackers can now go to websites and download protocols, programs and scripts to use against their victims.

Cyberterrorism: This is the premeditated, politically motivated attack against information, computer systems, computer programs, and data which result in violence against noncombatant targets. We shall discuss cyberterrorism as a separate topic as this is an area of special concern and because certain countries have legislated on the topic.

Industrial espionage: This is where corporations spy on other companies and with network systems; this can be an easy task. Companies can retrieve sensitive information rarely leaving behind any evidence. Cyberespionage can also be applied to nations that spy on other countries' sensitive information.

Spoofing of IP addresses. This is where a false IP address is used to impersonate an authorized user.

The reproduction and distribution of copyright protected material and software piracy

Cyberattacks on financial systems: This includes electronic banking and payment systems.

Cybervandalism: The defacing of webpages.

Pyramid schemes on the Internet.

E-mail abuse: This includes malicious or false e-mail.

Denial of service attacks.

Who are the local enforcers – what type of enforcement do we have in Malaysia?

Cyberlaw enforcers face several challenges:

Firstly, there is the identification of the criminal – Internet investigations are equipment- and labor-intensive. It is not that easy to identify cybercriminals.

This is because they operate in a virtual world and do not leave physical clues and paper trails behind, like the more traditional criminals do. Although they do leave their digital fingerprints now and then, enforcers need to move quickly before evidence fades away. Furthermore, with encryption, route relay and other types of technology and processes, they can make themselves almost undetectable by cyberenforcers.

Secondly, if the cybercriminal was in another country and he perpetrated his crimes against information systems here in Malaysia, how do you prosecute and ultimately impose the sentence against him? This is where the harmonization of a framework of cyberlaw globally will undoubtedly help (this was discussed in the Cyberlaws column in In.Tech, April 22. It is also the objective in respect to cyberlaw in the second phase of the MSC's development from 2003 to 2010), as the Internet is borderless and does not have regard to the laws of sovereign nations.

Insufficient Personnel

Besides legal differences, there are practical differences in terms of enforcement and co-ordination efforts between nations. There may not be enough trained personnel or sufficient equipment to detect and to bring cybercriminals to book.

Finally, technology always evolves and the enforcers must keep up with changes. Even in the United States as recently as 2000, it was noted that American law enforcement agencies, including the Justice Department, lacked the staff to investigate and prosecute cybercrimes like digital break-ins, data destruction and viruses. As a result of this, cybercriminals were breaking into or paralyzing US-based websites with little fear of retribution, costing the private sector hundreds of millions of dollars.

Even Interpol, the organization set up to track fugitives and investigate international crime and of which Malaysia is a member of, considered letting a Silicon Valley computer security company, AtomicTangerine, help it to protect businesses from hackers. This is after it acknowledged that international law enforcers were unable to combat computer crime effectively and also after acknowledging that governments found it difficult to coordinate cross-border efforts to combat this new phenomenon. Its secretary general at the time, Raymond Kendall stated that "... there's a limit to how you can transform police officers or detectives into technicians" (http://lists.insecure.org/lists/isn/2000/Jul/0056.html).

In Malaysia, the Malaysian Police formed the Technology Crime Investigation Branch (TCIB) in

October 1998. It is under the Commercial Crime Investigation Division. The officers in the TCIB are specially trained in cybercriminal investigation methods. The TCIB also lends its assistance to overseas enforcement agencies in investigating online gambling, hacking and illegal distribution of pirated software.

Here are a couple of tips on how to prevent cybercrime:

- Install hardware and software that will recognise hacker attacks, data spying and data altering, like firewalls, encryption (for e-mail, the encryption program called Pretty Good Privacy can be used), virus detection and smartcards. An Intrusion Detection System can protect your information systems in the event of the failure of the firewall and from internal attacks. An Incident Handling System will be able to identify hacker attacks as they happen. Full backups are important so that evidence like damaged or altered files, files left by the intruder, the relevant IP address and login times can be collected. A police report should then be made.

- Assess your information systems to identify weaknesses.

- Ensure that computers that run critical infrastructure are not physically connected to any other computer that is possibly connected to the Internet.

- Maintain clear and consistent security policies and procedures.

- Use alphanumeric passwords (i.e. passwords with letters and numbers in them). Login passwords should be changed frequently.

- Employees have to be trained to understand security risks – this practically means that they must know that they should never give out PINs, passwords and calling card numbers of the company without proper third party verification.

Notorious hacker, Kevin Mitnick, who was the most wanted hacker at one time in the United States, told of how he accessed the information systems of the US' Department of Motor Vehicles by simply calling up an officer, disguising himself as an officer from another government agency and obtaining the appropriate username and passwords from her.

- Correct identified problems – although this may seem straightforward and logical, I have seen many cases where security of certain information systems were compromised because problems were not fixed.

- Report attacks to the National ICT Security and Emergency Response Centre (Niser) so that any pattern of cybercrime in Malaysia can be detected and large-scale attacks prevented.

- There must exist incident response capabilities so that there is appropriate action taken against impending attacks.

- When an employee resigns or is terminated, employers must always ensure that the former does not have access to their computers anymore. The 1997 UN Manual on the Prevention and Control of Computer-Related Crime noted that 90% of economic crimes such as theft of information and fraud were committed by the relevant company's employees. Even the Malaysian Police's Technology Crime Investigation Branch is of the opinion that "more often than not, unauthorized access, hacking or e-mail abuse cases involve disgruntled employees taking advantage of ineffective security policies."

- Maintain backups of all important data.

- When external persons service your system, save confidential information on other media before the service. Observe them during the service. Never let external people take computers or servers with confidential information from your site.

Conclusion

In a speech in Kuala Lumpur in February 2000, Deputy Prime Minister Datuk Seri Abdullah Ahmad Badawi stated that: "The development of the Multimedia Super Corridor and the creation of a pioneer legal and regulatory framework encompassing, amongst other things, the Communications and Multimedia Act, the Computer Crimes Act and the Digital Signatures Act is indicative of the Government's commitment towards the creation of a knowledge-based economy." *(The Harvard Business School Alumni Club luncheon talk on Managing Malaysia in the New Global Economy.)*

Thus, the Computer Crimes Act must be seen not only as a law which regulates the behavior of people who use and do business over the Internet, but it also must be seen as the Government's efforts to put in place soft infrastructure to nurture the MSC and the knowledge-based economy so that Malaysia can achieve Vision 2020. At the same time, the Government should be aware that technological innovation and the deviousness of human minds would mean that the law as well as enforcement must not only keep up with cybercriminals, but it must ensure that their officers are one step ahead of cybercriminals, ready to catch them if the cybercriminals perform their dirty deeds.

Chapter 4 – I Have a Special Gift for My Readers

I appreciate my readers for without them I am just another author attempting to make a difference. If my book has made a favorable impression please leave me an honest review. Thank you in advance for you participation.

My readers and I have in common a passion for the written word as well as the desire to learn and grow from books.

My special offer to you is a massive ebook library that I have compiled over the years. It contains hundreds of fiction and non-fiction ebooks in Adobe Acrobat PDF format as well as the Greek classics and old literary classics too.

In fact, this library is so massive to completely download the entire library will require over 5 GBs open on your desktop.

Use the link below and scan all of the ebooks in the library. You can select the ebooks you want individually or download the entire library.

The link below does not expire after a given time period so you are free to return for more books rather than clog your desktop. And feel free to give the link to your friends who enjoy reading too.

I thank you for reading my book and hope if you are pleased that you will leave me an honest review so that I can improve my work and or write books that appeal to your interests.

Okay, here is the link…

http://tinyurl.com/special-readers-promo

PS: If you wish to reach me personally for any reason you may simply write to mailto:support@epubwealth.com.

I answer all of my emails so rest assured I will respond.

NOTE: All of the downloadable files in the massive ebook library have been scanned by eSet.com NOD 32 Antivirus 5 and are virus free!

ForensicsNation
435-249-5600
support@forensicsnation.com
http://www.forensicsnation.com

Meet the Author

Dr. Leland Benton is Director of Applied Web Info, a holding company for ePubWealth.com, a leading ePublisher company based in Utah. With over 21,000 resellers in over 22-countries, ePubWealth.com is a leader in ePublishing, book promotion, and ebook marketing.

As the creator and author of "The ePubWealth Program," Leland teaches up-and-coming authors the ins-and-outs of today's ePublishing world. He has assisted hundreds of authors make it big in the ePublishing world.

Leland also created a series of external book promotion programs and teaches authors how to promote their books using external marketing sources.

Leland is also the Managing Director of Applied Mind Sciences, the company's mind research unit and Chief Forensics Investigator for the company's ForensicsNation unit. He is active in privacy rights through the company's PrivacyNations unit and is an expert in survival planning and disaster relief through the company's SurvivalNations unit.

Leland resides in Southern Utah.

Visit some of his websites
http://www.AddMeInNow.com
http://www.AppliedMindSciences.com
http://www.BookbuilderPLUS.com
http://www.BookJumping.com
http://www.EmailNations.com
http://www.EmbarrassingProblemsFix.com
http://www.ePubWealth.com
http://www.ForensicsNation.com
http://www.ForensicsNationStore.com
http://www.FreebiesNation.com
http://www.HealthFitnessWellnessNation.com
http://www.Neternatives.com
http://www.PrivacyNations.com
http://www.RetireWithoutMoney.org
http://www.SurvivalNations.com
http://www.TheBentonKitchen.com
http://www.Theolegions.org
http://www.VideoBookbuilder.com

www.ingramcontent.com/pod-product-compliance
Lightning Source LLC
Chambersburg PA
CBHW051820170526
45167CB00005B/2097